happy are those

ancient wisdom for modern life

by

heather choate davis

HAPPY ARE THOSE:
ANCIENT WISDOM FOR MODERN LIFE.

ISBN: 978-0-9907642-4-3

heatherchoatedavis.com

happy are those

This small guidebook endeavors to look with 21st-century eyes at the wisdom of an ancient poem called the first psalm. It is often referred to as The Two Ways of Living and is likely the first self-help verse ever written. A psalm is a sung prayer born of the Hebrew people that lives on today in the Judeo-Christian tradition. If you consider yourself to be a "spiritual but not religious" person, you will find in this brief poem unexpected treasure. If you seek a better understanding of happiness but want no part of God, you will discover surprising wisdom in these words. People the world over have been happening upon them for many thousands of years and come away grateful. Maybe the reason this psalm endures is that the human heart never really changes, and forever leaps to find that happiness is close at hand. Whatever it is that you're looking for, may you find it in this prayer.

Happy are those
who do not follow the advice of the wicked,
or take the path that sinners tread,
or sit in the seat of scoffers;
but their delight is in the law of the LORD,
and on his law they meditate day and night.

They are like trees
planted by streams of water,
which yield their fruit in its season,
and their leaves do not wither.
In all that they do, they prosper.

The wicked are not so,
but are like chaff that the wind drives away.

Therefore the wicked will not stand in the
judgment, nor sinners in the congregation of the
righteous; for the LORD watches over
the way of the righteous,
but the way of the wicked will perish.

1

happy are those

Just say the word and you can feel it in your very bones, the presence or the absence of it: **happy**. Happiness is tied to the human heart, the human spirit, and the universal human search for the meaning of life. For most of human history, **happy** was intimately tethered to the wisdom of God, but today psychology and philosophy have stepped in to help us discover the root truths of happiness free from the burden of faith.

Martin Seligman, a leading 21st-century researcher in positive psychology describes happiness as having three parts: pleasure, engagement, and meaning. Pleasure is the "feel good" part of happiness. Engagement refers to living a "good life" of work, family, friends, and hobbies. Meaning refers to using our strengths to contribute to a larger purpose—to making an impact for good in the world. Seligman says that all three are important, but that of the three, engagement and meaning make the most difference in living a **happy** life.

With all this clarity about the nature of happiness it's curious, then, that our modern era is so filled with people suffering from depression, anxiety, isolation, despair, hopelessness, purposelessness, and feelings of deep insignificance. Maybe our love of individualism has made healthy engagement in community impossible. Maybe the sea of competitiveness we've created for ourselves to swim in has forced meaning to the back burner. Or perhaps we've been extracting happiness more from pleasure than engagement or meaning, undermining all three. How many of us find ourselves overdoing some "guilty pleasure" until it starts creating more guilt, boredom, or destruction than delight?

The road to happiness was never easy, but it was always clear.

who do not follow the advice of the wicked

This is the very first line of the very first psalm, an ancient form of sung poetry that serves as a bridge between the human heart and God. From the opening words the psalmist declares that happiness is a choice. We can choose to be happy or we can choose not to be happy. Or, as Abraham Lincoln claimed, "most people are about as happy as they make up their minds to be."

Bootstrap wisdom like this may serve to make a happy person feel smug, but to those who've lost sight of happiness, it feels like a kick in the teeth. Being told it's all on us always does. No, the psalmist's first word on choosing happiness is not some grand plan or program, but simply this: be careful who you listen to. In other words, do not follow the advice of the wicked.

Modern ears cannot bear to hear this word **wicked** unless it's in the context of entertainment: cackling witches, demonic cabals, nefarious extravaganzas that we can turn on and off with our remote control. *The Oxford English Dictionary* defines wicked as "evil or morally wrong; intended to or capable of harming someone or something." This is helpful. Because implicit in this secular definition is the idea that there *is* some objective standard of right and wrong, and that wrong views or actions cause harm. This is why the radically successful 12-step movement includes "making a searching and fearless moral inventory of ourselves" a part of its path to recovery: they know there can be no happiness when we are persistently hurting others.

As we now live in a culture that understands a posture of love as the belief that we're all basically "good people," we tend to recoil at the sound of anything that seems to label someone as a "bad" person. But look again: the purpose of the psalmist's words is not to judge a person but rather to protect you from their advice, which is—by definition—not moral, and by consequence, harmful.

As children, learning to recognize the advice of the wicked and the inevitable results of following it is one of our primary developmental tasks. As adults, this sorting process grows far murkier.

So what might the advice of the wicked look like in the 21st-century "grown-up" world? Well, it might take the form of a boss making relentless demands on a worker's time, tethering job security to round-the-clock availability, promising rewards that never come. The advice of the wicked might be the daily onslaught of media messages assuring us that as soon as we offer up our credit card for this year's fill-in-the-blank panacea that happiness will be ours. The advice of the wicked might be the voices shouting in the ear of fledgling adults that who they are is just not cutting it; that they simply aren't enough and, at this rate, never will be.

They're insidious, these messages, and well disguised as having our best interest at heart. They never promise a good life—no, let's leave that for the little people—but rather a Great Life. A Wikipedia-worthy life. A shareable, picture-perfect life. No matter the brass ring of the day, the outcome is always the same: following the advice of the wicked does not lead to happiness. It leads, inevitably, to pain.

But this really doesn't apply to you, right? You're not a follower—you're a leader! We're all leaders. The whole modern world of us determined to do anything but follow. Well, as much as we love to think that we are the great pioneers of our own lives this is never actually the case. Even the most entrepreneurial among us are actually following one of two opposing philosophies: "follow the money" or "do what you love and the money will follow." The dividing line is clear.

This is not to say that those who follow money are evil and those who follow love are good—far from it. A non-profit organization relies on the generosity of people of material wealth to empower its good work. In contrast, doing what one loves is not inherently noble; it is oftentimes little more than self-absorbed behavior that adds nothing to the common good.

What the psalmist reveals to us in the word **follow** is that our lives are sequences of movement and that these movements are headed in some direction, guided by some voice. The things we pursue or reject represent a path unseen, just under the surface. These two paths were here long before we came on the scene, and will carry on long after we're gone.

So we set out, determined to chart our own course. Before long we encounter some obstacle and turn to friends, family, and experts to help us navigate. This is where the truth of the two paths becomes clear: the advice we choose to follow will be that which aligns with the path we're already on, the form of happiness we seek, and the level to which we're invested in that particular path. This is true whether we recognize it or not.

###

Happy are those who do not follow
the advice of the wicked,

or take the path that sinners tread

"Two roads diverged in a yellow wood, and sorry I could not travel both, and be one traveler, long I stood." So begins Robert Frost's legendary poem *The Road Not Taken.* Considered by most to be a celebration of individuality and free thinking, the poem was actually intended by Frost to be a poetic mocking of one man's indecision, doubt, and tendency toward regret—the inward mechanism that keeps so many of us immobilized in our decision making, and forever looking back with "if only" on our lips.

This fear is rooted in the looming realization that our choices shape a timeline that cannot be wiped clean. We can move from Minneapolis to L.A. and back again, but we cannot rewrite our narrative as if we'd never been away. By going away, we come to recognize the very real possibility that we won't be coming back. Time wasted cannot be reclaimed. Bridges burned cannot be rebuilt. We are, as Frost reminds us, "one traveler" and our lives a series of roads diverging.

Contemporary thought now spins in a closed loop that tells us that the path to happiness is to follow our dreams, and realizing them is the visible proof that we are—tada!—officially happy. According to this new paradigm, we'd have to be, right?

Knowing well the folly and snare of this thinking, the psalmist directs us to an answer we don't want to hear: that the place where the paths of our lives diverge is at the center of the human heart, which is forever drawn towards self-interest. What the psalmist wants us to understand is that at every stage and quandary of our lives, we can either choose to connect more fully to the engagement and meaning forms of happiness, delighting in the pleasures planted within, or we can choose to cling (just a little longer please) to our own secret pleasure forms of happiness, at the expense of those we are meant to engage with, and find meaning and purpose in, with, and through. The next time you hole up in your room binging on episodic TV, social media, games—or worse—while flesh and blood people wait longingly on the other side of the door, you may see this divergence more clearly.

Now, a little time out is not the problem. Chronic self-indulgence is. This is the path that sinners tread and if you haven't already closed this book you are likely tempted. If there's anything we hate more than the sound of wicked it's **sinners**, a word we now reject outright as a form of judgment.

This wasn't always the case. In fact, it was never the case. For the whole of human history, every tribe and nation of the world, both secular and religious, recognized **sin** as the central flaw in the human condition, and used this understanding to bring reconciliation and healing to people and communities.

Apparently the shelf life for this wisdom is two thousand years. As we entered the 21st-century we decided that rejecting the kind of God who uses words like **sin** makes us freer, more loving people. That seems a worthy end, but sometimes these things need to play out before we understand the cost. We can see it now.

What we've lost on this new path of love is a way to look reality in the eye and still be able to live with ourselves, and with those we cannot find it in ourselves to understand or forgive. Now, instead of a consummate honesty, we worship a god called *transparency*, unaware that this new savior has risen up out of the void once filled with the truth revealed in sin.

Many today think of sin as "a Christian thing" but it is not. Socrates, the great Greek philosopher speaks of sin as the "disease of injustice," because it always takes its toll on innocents. The Ancient Jews upheld that a communal commitment to helping one another resist and atone for the perpetual lure of sin was essential for the health and happiness of the community. The goal was not to crush or dispirit or hold in contempt the human heart but, rather, to look at it unflinchingly: we are creatures that are perpetually drawn to having our own way. Pride convinces us that we are uniquely deserving of it. This self-centered tendency is called sin. Because of the incessant impulses we all have as people prone to sin (aka **sinners**), we need love in the form of both compassion and candor to help us navigate our lives. This is the big-picture, two path wisdom of which the psalmist speaks.

So where did our modern denial begin? Well, as we neared the end of the 20th century, the explosive and combined energies of the sexual revolution, the resentments of oppressed churchgoers, and the irresistible freedom of oral contraceptives joined forces. The timeless understanding of sin as "our self-centered natures at odds with the needs of others" was reframed as sin as "vices." Not who we are, but what we do.

This was a game changer because now we were off the hook! These "little things" that were supposedly so bad were suddenly viewed in a new light: who says? With rebellious hearts we shouted that the source of the problem was not us, but whoever made the list—and the floodgates flew open. We were heady with love and peace and lust—the great liberation—allowing our commitment to the fabric of daily human relations to become a shrug: I'll tolerate your thing, if you tolerate mine. In a matter of decades, this came to be our cultural understanding of what real love should look like.

So now when we're enticed by some great pleasure—despite a clear downside of hurting others—we are free to throw up our hands without shame, "the heart wants what the heart wants." This bit of pop philosophy comes from the contemporary filmmaker, Woody Allen, but there is no revelation in his claim. It has always been true that the heart wants what the heart wants. What is new is the notion that because the heart wants what the heart wants it is not only entitled to have it, but that this very wanting and having should now be promoted as a virtue.

The artist's life gives us a chance to consider the psalmist's advice. Let's say that the heart wants to be an actress. The divergence is not about whether being an actress is a "good" or "bad" thing, or whether or not one should or should not be an actress. If the rising up in the heart comes from a place of giftedness and calling, if it leads a young woman to apply herself to study and practice, to make sacrifices and develop discipline, to be called into a community where she can participate in both engagement and meaning, then, despite the inevitable rejections and hardships, this can be a happy path.

But let's remember, the path is not about a career but the bent of our choices. If the actress marries, for example, how will a life of late night rehearsals, distant locations, and frequent, often intimate, interactions with other men impact the promises she's made to her husband? All hearts are easily swayed by flirtation and the thrill of the new. A few drinks in a dark corner and the advice of the wicked will roar, "but the heart wants what the heart wants!" Before she knows what hit her—or claims to—she will be distancing herself from her first love, undermining the happiness they had once enjoyed through their shared engagement, and the richness of meaning that is found in a lasting union that endures through these inevitable temptations. Were the psalmist at the bar that night he would have said, "Walk away. It's not worth it."

Pleasure is a hard habit to break. Each time we choose to indulge our own desires at the expense of a friend or co-worker or spouse or child, we increase the chances that we'll do it again. Before long, the actress has a new spouse, new exes, new sets of scattered kids. Her heart longs now for a little time to curl up, to turn back, to feel at peace with the flesh of her flesh—that first pure heart place where pleasure and engagement and meaning kiss—but a staff of handlers advises her to take the work while she can. She's not getting any younger.

This is the inescapable truth of which the psalmist sings: the path that sinners tread is a dead end.

###

Happy are those
who do not follow
the advice of the wicked,
or take the path that sinners tread,

or sit in the seat of scoffers

Daily in America we bemoan the state of our political gridlock, the flippant talking-point chatter of our news media, the culture of cynicism and snark that reigns in our social media landscape. We point our mad fingers as if we have no part it in, unable to see that the scorn is us, the contempt is us—we who have made a throne of the seat of **scoffers**. The psalmist shows us that this is the inevitable destination of those who venture along the path of the wicked until, ultimately, we settle in, get comfortable, put our feet up. "You, idiot!" We could watch this show all day.

Modern psychology gives us terms like *social identity theory*, *social comparison theory*, and *ego threat* to describe behaviors that any one of us knows first hand from the playground. Putting other people down is an easy path to popularity. Any child can see that a snide remark directed towards a vulnerable peer elicits instant glee from the pack. The child no doubt feels a deep pang of remorse, but those guilt feelings are quickly overwhelmed by the joviality and approval of the **scoffers**. Approval seeking at the expense of another used to fade for most with age, but our daily backdrop of reality television, frenemy culture, and the lucrative industry of outrage seem to be delaying that milestone.

How, then, are we to live in peace in a world of "us and them?" Let's begin by recognizing that our "who's in and who's out" behavior is as ancient as the psalms. We are born to be a part of something larger than ourselves, and that larger connection comes through relationships with others. Since we can't all be part of the same group or gathering, some measure of comparison enters in. Is group A better than group B by some objective standard, or do I come to believe that my group is better merely because that's the one where I find myself? Investment begets loyalty and loyalty leads to tribalism, which, in and of itself, is not the scoffer's seat.

Let's consider the tradition of the sports rivalry. Many enjoy rooting and cheering and boasting about their favorite teams. They derive almost as much pleasure in good-naturedly sparring with friends or acquaintances that favor a rival team. This playful competition can unite people, actually building relationships where there is, on the surface, division. But when agitated fans begin beating one another up in the parking lot after a game, it is clear we are no longer on the right road.

How we choose to think, act, and speak about those who belong to a competing tribe or hold contradictory views from our own, this is the turf of the psalmist's teaching. The **scoffer** is one who speaks with contempt and derision about people and their ideas. The **scoffer** takes the stance that certain people and ideas are worthless or despicable. The **scoffer** shouts that certain people and their ideas are not worthy of his consideration. The **scoffer** makes this clear by mocking the person's name, views, history, beliefs, until there is no humanity left in them. Until they are the butt of a joke, nothing more. This is the **scoffer's** victory.

Who among us is not guilty of being the **scoffer** at some time, in some way, or to some extent? The psalmist is holding a mirror up to the darkness in our own hearts so that we may see the path we're on. So that we may catch ourselves and turn back. This option is open to any one of us who dares to see ourselves in this verse. To anyone who feels the gut check of careless words, rigid views, mocking spirits. It is only when we believe that the psalmist's truths do not apply to us—that our scoffing has nothing to do with wickedness and everything to do with our own superiority—that our chance of finding happiness is lost.

Life, as the psalmist reminds us, is a series of movements, heading in a direction. Life, like wind and breath and blood, moves. Life on the path of happiness grows, shifts, stumbles, retreats, blossoms.

In the seat of scoffers, we are no longer headed anywhere but deeper down in the place where we've chosen to hunker—like trolls. We imagine our defiant posture is bold and original when, in truth, we are living out the oldest tale in the book, destined to become, in the immortal words of Joni Mitchell, "cynical and drunk and boring someone in some dark café."

Choose to lift people up

2

But their delight is in the law of the Lord

From the origin of pulse and breath and longing, **delight** has been a part of the human experience. The garden in which the narrative of God's relationship to mankind begins is, tellingly, named delight (i.e., Eden). Far from a goody-two-shoes kind of happiness, **delight** is pleasure of the highest order. How could it not be, with its Latin roots including both *desire* and *allure*? Desire and allure. Allure and desire. Can you see the dance? What we long for in our innermost beings turns out to be one and the same as that which entices us. **Delight** is the point where allure and desire make fireworks.

Our understanding of *desire* and *allure* today is often limited to sex. As gratifying as sex may be in the moment, it doesn't come close to the delight of which the psalmist speaks. Much like stars in a city full of neon lights, the gift of true delight has been drowned out in the new world order, where desire is a commodity, and we, its eager consumers. In the absence of God, sexual desire has promoted itself to the be-all and end-all of pleasure, leaving us with a landscape of shadowy souls still trying to find themselves—and market themselves as desirable—well into old age.

The psalmist sings of a very different kind of **delight**. The kind that whispers in our ear and leads us to the place where, according to Frederick Buechner, "our deep gladness and the world's great hunger meet." This divine intersection of meaning, purpose, and pleasure is considered by most to be the highest and best life one could hope for but increasingly we've divorced ourselves from the source.

If we thought about it, we'd realize that this whole idea of "meant to be" doesn't make much sense without a One who meant it, but mostly we don't want to think about that. We don't want some dinosaur idea of a happy life; we want a totally new and thoroughly, passion-filled life of our own creation! More often than not, we're not entirely sure what it is we're passionate about but we know passion is key. Passion is code for "something I not only love but was born to do." Passion is the new vocation.

And so we set out, patching together whatever pieces of pleasure and success we can only to discover that the desire to find one's passion is not, as it turns out, the same as finding it. Maybe it's because our choices invariably skew toward the quick fix or the feel-good. Or that we dismiss unlikely doors outright, oblivious to the hidden treasures just on the other side. Or that, ultimately, passions aren't found but rather unearthed, a process that requires both humility and pain, which we tend to avoid at all costs.

Delight operates on a different plane. God knows long before we do what our deep gladness is, and the ten thousand often circuitous and confounding steps that will lead us, measure by measure, to that cosmic fit. This place of delight is not one fixed role or job or mission, but rather a path that changes and morphs with time and circumstance, held together by nothing more than our willingness to trust that he has our best interest at heart in all things. Sometimes this is hard to see. We are often tested beyond our ability to believe. Even when we think we're listening, we lose our way. No worries. The first psalm waits patiently to show us the way back.

And the way back is not at all what we expect. The same God who reveals to us a level of delight we may have given up hoping for claims we'll find this delight—our very heart's desire—in his law. Nothing about this sounds right. Even the pairing of those two words—**delight**, so lush and luminous, and **law**, so rigid and imposing—feels like a disconnect. Until we come to see that our understanding of the law of the Lord is as narrow as our definition of delight.

Modern ears tend to hear phrases like the **law of the Lord** to mean rules, judgment, and punishment. We don't seem to have the same problem with phrases like the law of gravity, the law of physics, or the law of nature. These we understand to mean proven concepts of how things are, of how they work—a reliable guide for the principles we see lived out in cause and effect every day. We do not balk about these laws because they seem to be true without referencing God. This is our modern gold standard for truth: let's leave God out of it.

Ok, so what if we thought of his law as **the law of us?** A reliable guide to human behavior intended to minimize suffering and maximize happiness for all people—with this parenthetical option: "as set forth by the one who created us all, and therefore knows how we operate." His "laws" are recognized across the spectrum of ideology and theology, and are consistent with natural law, philosophy, sociology, psychology and a human understanding of goodness. Rare is the culture, for example, that fails to recognize that murder and robbery are immoral and unjust. Greed and covetousness—be it someone's bigger house, better job, more attractive spouse—are universally recognized as a slippery slope.

This is our most common modern predicament, perpetually wanting what someone else has. Never feeling that we are, have, or will ever be enough. In the event that we do achieve the coveted whatever, we find ourselves terrified of losing it and overwhelmed by feelings that we never really deserved it anyway. By no standard would a person in this state be considered happy.

This is where **the law of us** (aka of the Lord) can shed a bit of unique light on the way of happiness. Like taking one day a week and using it to do nothing but be. To consider, perhaps, that the whole of the world does not rest on our shoulders. That there may be some wisdom that our advanced technology has not, in fact, made obsolete.

Our digitally-addicted, work-glutted, anxiety-ridden era is starved for this undergirding principle of abiding peace, unaware that we brought the need on ourselves when we looped God out of the conversation. So now we try to life-hack and backfill our way to some feeling of reassurance, some counterpoint to our gnawing suspicion that there's something terribly wrong. Please tell us that if we just do this, this, and this, we're going to be ok we plead—if not in words, than in click-thrus. And the market is happy to oblige, lavishing us with platforms promoting kindness and empathy and that most celebrated of good things: gratitude.

Few of us think of gratitude as a religious word anymore but it actually comes to us through **grace**, the word God uses for his gift of unconditional love. The whole Sunday morning thing? It's really just a thank-you note for the promise of being loved no matter what. Unlike our modern understanding of gratitude—which looks around at all the wonderful things we have and says with something like reverence, gosh, I'm glad I've got all this—the essence of gratitude recognizes the giver. This is the purpose of **the law of the Lord**: to lead us back to the heart of the God who sees right through us and delights in us anyway.

###

But their delight
is in the law of the Lord

and on his law
they meditate
day and night

We humans love to group ideas, practices, and people by word associations. It helps us make sense of where things belong. In its simplest form, it tells us if something is "like us" or "like them." The word **meditate** has become such a word. Meditation is something that we currently think of as belonging to the practice of Buddhism, or Hinduism, or the kind of yoga that makes breathing a form of prayer. "They" wouldn't call it *prayer,* though, because those who steer clear of the psalmist's God think of *prayer* as a "them" word, just as those who claim *prayer* as an "us" word are leery of the word **meditate**.

Yet, there it is. Right there in the first psalm. God's best advice for how we—as in all of us—are to attain happiness. We are to **meditate.** To contemplate, to consider. In the realm of the psalmist, this means we are to ponder what God is trying to teach us about life.

As far back as the 3rd century, followers of the Living God have turned to the Scriptures to find divine wisdom greater than the sum of the words alone. By the 6th century, many would devote themselves to a practice known as *lectio divina*, or, divine reading.

This practice begins by reading not for the literal understanding of the words or passages but as a form of listening. Reading with the ears of the heart. Once a word or passage begins to "speak" to us, we then take it in and meditate on it. The ancient image was of rumination, as a cow "chews on" the grasses of the field, turning them over and over, slowly extracting the juice from each blade. In this process of meditation, we allow our own personal challenges, wounds, memories and desires to intersect with the word of God, the wisdom of God—his law—as it draws us into deeper understanding, peace, and wholeness.

But who could possibly meditate **day and night**? No one has that kind of time anymore. Well, unlike the 21st-century start-up manager, God is not a slave driver. Over the years, those who have ruminated prayerfully on this verse have discovered many layers of meaning in the phrase **day and night.**

For example, it may be a poet's shorthand for the beginning and end of each day. The psalmist might be saying that **happy are those** who start each day with the word of God, considering how it might apply to the human interactions we will have, the activities we will engage in, the decisions we will need to make, and then, at the end of the day, reflecting on how we were able to see God at work in our lives. What modern ears leap to interpret—and therefore dismiss—as a call to be on our knees 24/7, may actually be more like the time it takes to brew a pot of coffee that leads one, step by step, to sustained **delight.**

Twentieth-century philosopher and mystic, Thomas Kelly, imagined in the psalmist's **day and night** our two distinct layers of mental activity. The foreground, where we organize, calculate, and work through the tasks of the day, and the background, where a gauzy scrim of prayer and contemplation may be humming just behind the scenes.

Still others have considered that the psalmist is reminding us to meditate on his law in good times and bad, where **day and night** represent to us both lightness and dark. Even if we are not inclined towards God, most of us have experienced times of despair or confusion pressing enough to make us cry out to someone we think might be powerful or merciful enough to help. What might happen if, in our searching, we were to take a few minutes to meditate on a verse like this:

> Blessed are the poor in spirit,
> for theirs is the kingdom of Heaven.

This is the opening line of a famous teaching called The Beatitudes. In many ways it's the companion verse to the first psalm because that's what *blessed* actually means—**happy**—and vice versa. Now, none of us is keen to imagine that happiness begins with being poor in spirit. That's because we start out with a preconceived idea of what we want it to look like—happiness—as opposed to a transformation of the heart that we allow.

So the question we need to ask ourselves is this: do we really want to be happy, or do we only want to have our version of what we think a good kind of happy would look like?

If it's actual, time-tested, mystery-charged happiness we seek, the psalmist invites us to take the words of these prayer poems in and see where they lead. In doing so we'll be joining today's busy monks, organic farmers, stay-at-home moms, hipster scholars, travelling executives, creators and coders, and grass roots movers and shakers who **meditate day and night** in just this way, slowly pondering these life-giving words, often times while brushing their teeth.

3
they are like trees planted

When we find ourselves humbled by nature, it is usually the unimaginable sweep of the oceans or the mocking heft of the mountains that brings us to our knees. In truth, we are more like trees, a single life, with roots in a given place that has the capacity for startling beauty. Have you ever seen a really old tree? Some have been alive and growing for five thousand years, with branches that gnarl and crimp and tell stories no modern man can recall. Few among us are not compelled to throw open our arms in awe at the sight of them. These **trees**, the psalmist sings, are a fixed witness to life, and they are intended as our model.

Leonardo da Vinci noticed something curious about trees over 500 years ago. Each and every branch has a direct, mathematical relationship to the branch from which it springs. And that relationship, modern physicists have now discovered, aligns precisely with the principles engineers use to help vertical structures accommodate airflow. Which is why the vast majority of live trees do not topple—even in 100-mile-an-hour winds.

This is what it means to be **planted.** Not merely passing through but *here*, fully present, where the planter has placed us. A tree planted is both firmly established in an environment and continuously alive and growing in that place. It is not a term of settling but rather of flourishing, of becoming what T.S. Eliot calls, "the still point of the turning world."

Although trees may grow in any number of settings, the psalmist points us to a very specific source for this human flourishing...

They are like trees planted,

by streams of water

Long before science could prove it, it was true: water never dies. The fluid of the first tear ever shed is still with us. The H_2O molecules in the blood of every person who every walked the earth are still with us. The water that became wine? Still with us. No matter what you may think or believe about God, there is no disputing the fact that water is life. And **streams of water** are a constant influx of this new and everlasting life.

When we thirst—physically, spiritually—it seems that we are crying out to relieve the deep dryness within but the cry is actually mutual. Just as it is with *desire* and *allure*, the water of life is actually calling out to us, tugging at our roots, which grope longingly in response for the source.

Trees planted beside streams of water have deep and every widening root systems seeking and burrowing below the surface. A tree perpetually drawing on life-giving water will itself become a source of life. What, then, do we imagine the psalmist is telling us that we, like trees planted, can become?

###

They are like trees
planted by streams of water,

which yield their fruit
in its season

What is the fruit of mankind? What is the fruit you or I were meant to bear? There is no tree on earth that exists for the purpose of yielding "bad" fruit; the essence of who we are and what we are created to bring forth is good. Good fruit takes time. It takes time and patience and discipline and care and a steady stream of living water. So we are born to yield good fruit, yes—but not every day. Not every week or month or even year. This is what **seasons** are all about.

As we neared the end of the 20th century, we began to view seasons as something to make an end run around. If the people wanted strawberries in December, well then we'd go where they grow strawberries in December and spray 'em and pack 'em and ice 'em and ship 'em and—voila! In our results-driven world, seasons are merely an obstacle to be bulldozed over. That we've traded in a natural lifecycle for a manufactured stream of tasteless fruit—shiny and deceptive and available on demand—is a consequence we have chosen to ignore.

A cry in the wilderness always brings us back to the truth. And so it is, in the early years of the 21st century, we see a return to the earth, to the garden, to the wisdom of seasons, to the local farmer's market and the glorious cycle of rutabagas in November and apricots in May, and a rising gratitude for one plump and perfectly sweetened plum in July. Composting is back in fashion, too, and with it the glory of decomposing, of the slow and teeming preparations that redeem our rubbish and fill our hands with the dank and heavy soil of new life.

The lessons of the **seasons** have been slower to return to our daily calendars. The November day we call black as a wink to the accountant's ledger is one example of how we turned a day of gratitude into a frenzied jumpstart on consumption. Course corrections are underway but these do not begin to touch the driving force behind it all: quarterly-earnings-report thinking pressing down and infecting every aspect of our existence. The reporting cycle of the business world makes us believe that we were built to perform impressively and at increasing levels in every three-month stretch of our lives. That not to do so is not only disappointing, but existential. That our value as people, as workers, as parents, as progeny depends on how good we all look on paper at all times.

Throughout the 150 prayer poems gathered together to form The Psalms, we hear of a different kind of life. A life of **seasons**. Seasons of joy and good fruit, to be sure. But also seasons of loss, of sadness, of failure; of uncertainty and rest; of illness and health; of seeking, pondering, raging, resurrecting; an ever-present cycle of death and new life meted out in due course across the landscape of our very human days.

Every time we encourage 10-year old boys to drop all sports but the one they're best at in the hopes that it might lead to some distant and mathematically impossible glory, we are rejecting the beauty of seasons; of playing football and soccer and basketball and baseball; of playing nothing at all; of playing even when they're not very good; of **seasons** of sport for no other reason than to feel the joy of their bodies moving like some well-built machine as their heart and pulse and spirit join with others in the celebration.

Every time we counsel 13-year old girls to spend their weekends cramming for tests to secure their place in some mandatory, unknowable future, we are denying them the **seasons** of bewilderment and soul-searching, of listening for the still small voice inside them rising up to declare itself and its right to sit by the water of life and say: show me.

These are the seasons that precede good fruit. In *its* season means when the time is right *for the fruit*—not for us. Given our primal, internal drive towards self-interest and the external pressures of a world hell-bent on measurable, monetized production, we now harbor an expectation that our lives should ceaselessly bear impressive evidence of worth.

As a salve to our weary souls, the psalmist offers this gentle reminder: no human being can generate anything of value day after day, year after year, no matter how tirelessly we labor. It goes against the very laws of nature. It goes against **the law of us**.

When we strive day and night to produce and win favor, the best we can hope for is a dull and hollowed out imitation, with a shiny photogenic peel, and nostalgia for a time we can longer quite name.

Herein lies the rub for young moderns who place work-life balance at the top of their list of priorities: it simply can't be found on the path that shouts Faster, Higher, More.

###

They are like trees
planted by streams of water,
which yield their fruit in its season,

and their leaves do not wither

This sounds like a bit of an overpromise, doesn't it? We all know that the **leaves** of trees do, in fact, wither, often changing glorious colors before falling and whispering reminders of death. So what is the psalmist trying to say when he compares us to trees with leaves that **do not wither**?

Let's start by considering what exactly withering is: a process of decline set in motion by a lack of moisture. We see it in our aging eyes, in the thinning skin of our hands. Moisture is a sign of youth, of newness, the fresh start of morning dew. Our eyes bear witness to the elemental truth that moisture is water and water is life.

When our lives become like trees planted by streams of water, it is our spirit which is ceaselessly quenched, internally renewing us even as our physical body reveals—much like the rings in a tree trunk—our accumulating years. Our leaves do not wither because living water roots us in hope, and hope always points to new life.

Restoring vitality is actually one of the essential properties of **leaves**. The leaves of the loquat, moringa, and carob trees, for example, can rid our bodies of toxins. The olive leaf is born to combat bacteria and infections. Bay leaves are a gift for the lessening of swelling and pain. And the leaves of the neem tree? Well, according to the U.S. National Library of Medicine, the "neem leaf and its constituents have been demonstrated to exhibit anti-inflammatory, antioxidant, antiviral, antiulcer, antimalarial, antihyperglycaemic, anticarcinogenic, antifungal, antibacterial, antimutagenic, and immunomodulatory properties." This wisdom is the good fruit of the laws of nature revealed in us, and recognized in both traditional and alternative medicine.

But the psalmist sings of something even more promising. When we spend day and night drawing on streams of living water, we become what **leaves** are by nature: healers. When our roots are connected to the source of life, we have within us the capacity to heal—not just occasionally, or when the moon is just right—but in every human interaction. Even in our own fallow seasons, we may play a part in healing others, emotionally, spiritually—sometimes even physically—that they, too, may become bearers of good fruit.

And always, **leaves** model for us the wisdom of community. Because each individual leaf is not only shaped to maximize its intake of sunlight (and therefore live out its energy-producing purpose to the fullest), it is carefully placed in relationship to the other leaves—a staggering of sorts—with which it shares a common stem, branch, and trunk. While human beings battle with zero-sum thinking (anything good for someone else is a loss for me), **leaves** teach us that it is actually possible to get more than enough sun without casting dark shadows on your neighbor. This communal approach to the work of the day is the secret to the enduring vitality of trees.

They are like trees
planted by streams of water,
which yield their fruit in its season,
and their leaves do not wither.

In all that they do, they prosper.

If we draw a line connecting the most desirable keywords we've seen so far it might look something like this: **happy** — **delight** — **prosper**. We sought happiness and discovered it was all about whom we listened to. This led us to find delight in the law of the Lord (aka the handbook for understanding life as put forth by the one who created it and therefore knows how things work). From there it's more a matter of logic than faith: the person who has the working manual for life is more likely to find success in it. We can, therefore, expect to see prosperity in their lives in the form of goals attained, honors bestowed, funding secured, health granted, and love actualized.

While these are all desirable things, they are only a part of what the psalmist means when he uses the word **prosper**. Unfortunately, we face two significant challenges today in embracing the fullness of the ancient's view. The first is this: when we decided to lay God off and promote ourselves to the Highest Authority in our own lives we ushered in the epoch of self-promotion. So whatever prosperity we feel we're entitled to is now entirely on us. In the social, global, and exponential reality of our 21st-century world, this means our prosperity is intimately tethered—one might even say shackled—to our willingness or ability to promote ourselves, and to create the perception that we're killing it.

You want seasons? Fine. There're a thousand other guys who are perfectly happy to go without 'em. (Well, not perfectly happy, but you get the idea). We hear about those who excel in prosperity hunting in our social media newsfeeds as they promote the fruit of their labors (or ask our help to fund them), which only increases the sense that who we are is somehow lacking.

The second challenge comes from many of the people who claim to speak for God in the modern era, promoting a version of truth called the "prosperity" Gospel. This is the movement that fuels much of the televangelism that keeps so many (you, perhaps?) from going anywhere near a church. The message is simple: God wants you to be rich. God wants you to have every single thing you ever wanted and if you just keep coming here and throwing money in the plate he's going to give it to you.

The psalmist has a word for this but it is not **prosper**. God promises prosperity in many forms but it is not found on a path of lies. It can't be. Because that path has no access to his even greater and more palpable gifts: our inner triumphs over the demons of fear, anxiety, envy, anger, hate, and despair as we wrestle outwardly with the world. To win these battles is to **prosper** in the fullest sense.

This holistic view of success comes from the same family of meaning as *shalom*. Peace. With oneself, with one's neighbor, and with God. In his poem, "Pax," D. H. Lawrence captures it like this:

...Sleeping on the hearth of the living world
yawning at home before the fire of life
feeling the presence of the living God
like a great reassurance
a deep calm in the heart
a presence
as of the master sitting
at the board in his own and greater being,
in the house of life.

Carrying this peace within us, we are free to move through our days without the constant gnaw and tug of not being enough. Free to live like a tree planted, with the quiet knowledge that we embody the seasons and that all we are and do will lead one way or another to human flourishing.

When we view prosperity as nothing more than a numbers game, peace will forever elude us. Stuck at the first booth of the midway, we toss our days away over some gaudy, top-shelf panda, never realizing (until the end, perhaps) that we’ve missed the main event.

4

The wicked are not so

This entire prayer poem is an expression of diametric opposites. We have just pondered all that the psalmist might mean when he speaks about our lives as trees planted by streams of water. Happy are those, he tells us. Blessed are those. Now we are faced with this hard word again—**wicked**—and in a context that says quite clearly that they are not like the people who are blessed.

What we need to remember before going a moment further is that none of us is all one thing or the other. We are, each one of us, at every minute, leaning in one direction or the other, and always, with the invitation or temptation to see or do it differently. That said, if those who are like trees planted beside streams of water are happy, that would seem to make **the wicked** "those destined to be unhappy."

Leo Tolstoy's timeless opening to *Anna Karenina* claims that, "Happy families are all alike; each unhappy family is unhappy in its own way." Written in Russia in the late 1800s, this book was selected in 2007 by a *Time* magazine poll of 125 contemporary authors as the greatest novel of all time. Because then, as now, there were happy families and there were unhappy families. And despite all our seeming differences, happy families now, as then, are remarkably alike. If we were to measure the arc of the days of a stadium full of happy 21st-century families, we would see amidst their glorious variation and totally human imperfection a single common thread: they make a habit of steering clear of behaviors and influences that cause harm to themselves and those around them.

Palliative caregiver Bronnie Ware considered the issue of happiness from another angle in a simple blog entitled *The Top 5 Regrets of the Dying*. Shared by over 3 million readers in its first year, her wisdom continues to live on in constant circulation through social media as well as in book form. People, it seems, are hungry for big picture truth—the kind that most never quite pinpoint until they recognize their path has run out. Caring for strangers in their final weeks, Bonnie found her own meaning and purpose in listening to the desires that people were never quite able to act on. The top five regrets were these:

1. I wish I'd had the courage to live a life true to myself, not the life others expected of me.
2. I wish I hadn't worked so hard.
3. I wish I'd had the courage to express my feelings.
4. I wish I had stayed in touch with my friends.
5. I wish that I had let myself be happier.

The first gives us much to ponder, drawing us back to the lessons of Robert Frost and the reminder that the road not taken is not about bold individualism, but rather, about regret. In their wish for more courage, we see within the dying a lifelong battle. They seem to have had a sense of "owing something," of being guided by other's voices and demands—an intimate twist on the advice of the **wicked**—which they followed all the way to the grave.

Now whether these opprcssive expectations were real or imagined, whether or not they were yielded to out of a sense of love or duty or fear or shame, the outcome is the same. At the very core of their being, many—far too many—of the dying felt they had not lived the life they were meant for.

Curiously, two of the five regrets speak of this absence of courage; of the strength of heart and will to say bravely to those we love that we thirst for purpose and meaning, that we need their help and support to find it, that we long to see them be **happy** in this same way.

Why do we find this so hard? Are we afraid of being rejected? Are we anxious about the inevitable changes this desire for authenticity might require? Are we terrified by the thought of what it might look like if we actually pursued happiness in some less obvious or enviable form—or let the people we share our lives with do the same?

At this point it might be easy to shout: see, this is why we shouldn't care so much about other people. This is why we shouldn't get married or have kids or do anything that will take us away from being who we truly are. Maybe. But the other regrets don't support this self-centered ideal.

When a person on their deathbed wishes that they'd spent less time working, it is almost always because they regret not having had more time with family and friends. If regret two doesn't make that clear, regret four certainly does. This is because we are built for community, and the fullness of close relationships meets our deepest needs more than anything else we could ever aspire to.

Notice that on a list of the five most common regrets, we don't see anyone wishing they'd made more money or had more sex or earned a more impressive title. The unrequited desire to travel the world didn't even make the list. And regretting how one handled a particular problem or challenge? None of this seems to matter in our final hours.

Which brings us to the end of the path of the **wicked**, which is peopled with those who generated or followed—or cowered to—credos that were not life giving. *I wish that I'd let myself be happier.* When our pulse grows faint, the truth of who or what we listened to becomes utterly transparent. If we've tried to find happiness by jumping through hoops, or making an altar of pleasure, or crouching down in the hopes that we might just slide in under the radar, it does not appear we get to leave this life in a state of *shalom*.

###

The wicked are not so,

but are like chaff

Most of us are so far removed from the elements of farming, that we have to stop and think: what, exactly, is **chaff**? Oh, yeah—that dry, thin part on the outside of the grain, the part that gets thrown away after the threshing. Again, the psalmist reveals that the condition of the wicked is one of dryness. There is no living water in **chaff**: therefore, it cannot be a source of life.

Modern ears struggle with these challenging parallels because they smack of absolutism. Our enlightened world prefers to greet each day with the cry that I can be life-giving chaff if I want to! We champion the right to have it both ways by spurning the idea of good or bad paths, people, or means.

But our rejection doesn't change the human heart or the lessons that our lives invariably teach—just our ability to learn from them.

Our rejection is based in part on who we envision these "happy" people to be. If we hear this psalm and think, this is saying that people who go to church are happy and people who don't are unhappy, then we need to broaden our thinking. The psalms, which were written long before Jesus walked the earth (and therefore, before anything known as the church even existed), are never this simplistic. They always reflect the great complexity of the human experience, a common element in all "wisdom literature."

And although the enduring truths of the psalms have been tested throughout history, they have never faced so great or omnipresent an adversary as the multi-media distortion of what God's people look, sound, and act like posturing loudly across a hundred channels, streams, and sites.

Let's just stop. Just for a moment. And block out all that noise.

Good.

Now, to be able to hear what the psalmist is saying, we need to erase any preconceptions we have of this threshing image and look at a truth that is likely to make all kinds of people unhappy: there is nearly as much **chaff** in the church as there is in the neighborhood coffee house. Because many who attend worship services are not actually like trees planted by streams of water. Despite their Sunday attendance, they live lives that demonstrate they are still following, primarily, **the advice of the**

wicked: shop, accumulate, condemn, compete, exclude.

Meanwhile, just down the street, there are those who may not know much about the law of the Lord but whose own heart's desire has led them to follow a path of peace, patience, kindness, goodness, steadfastness, compassion, discipline and love. People who, in the process of leaning into their own God-given lives, have come to embody **the way of the blessed** without even knowing its name.

So the **chaff** of which the psalmist sings is not a person who does not go to church, but, rather, a person who is so drained from trying to have their own way, or looking for happiness where none is to be found, that they have nothing left in them.

They are most noticeable in two distinct forms. On the one hand, there is the **chaff** that is brittle and famished at the core, highly susceptible to the modern predicament of "bright, shiny, object" disease, and looking for any new thing to slake their thirst. Someone who continually makes choices that feel to them like the happiness they deserve, but which leave them and everyone around them depleted.

On the other hand, there is the **chaff** whose dryness is a form of constipation. Faced with even a breath of change, they grow tighter, harder and more resistant. Threatened by what they see as an attack on their way of happiness—the right way, the only way—their behavior mirrors fear and self-righteousness far more than the psalmist's delight.

These are just two extremes on a spectrum of self-made drought. There are many other forms; as many ways, in fact, to become like chaff as there are to become unhappy. **Wicked** is the psalmist's shorthand for them all.

###

the wicked are not so,
but are like chaff

that the wind drives away

No one knows where the wind comes from or where it goes. Sure, modern meteorology can tell us about the winds coming in off the ocean or the desert, but a sudden gust of wind is always just that: sudden. It brings with it an element of surprise. Wind, by its very nature, is a change agent, stirring things up, moving things around, not only in the visible world but also in us.

The "winds of change" is a global image of transformation, but here the psalmist applies it to the withered heart of the chaff. This chaff is to be lifted up and **driven**

away from the center of life, the natural consequence of a persistent pattern of choices. This would seem an irreversible verdict, until we look upon this phrase with new eyes. Notice that the psalmist doesn't say destroyed, pulverized, or torched. These would be words of finality but he does not use those here.

Instead, he sets the **chaff** in flight, knowing that any force capable of driving it away is capable of transforming it. One slight turn—one honest cry for help—and that dry soul may indeed be given a way to live on, to become some new thing; a shower of manna, perhaps. An oasis, even, that someday others might find life-giving water and rest in their presence.

Have you ever heard of the Holy Spirit? It's the face of the Living God that moves like the wind, changing hearts and the way we see things. The Holy Spirit is the mysterious force that brings life where there is no life—to chaff, to the wicked, and especially, to the unhappy.

On this you can rely. When the psalmist tells us that the wicked are like chaff that the wind drives away, here is what he is whispering beneath the words: *and a rushing wind can change your life if you let it.*

5

Therefore the wicked will not stand in the judgment

Pick a day—any day—and you will have to make a judgment call. A teenager will need to decide whether or not it's worse to cheat on a test or to get a bad grade (the majority now decide that cheating is better). Parents of young children will either give into a child's demands for a treat or hold firm on the more demanding work of teaching them to delay those desires (we tend to be very clear on when others are weak in this area, less so when we are). In a competitive workplace, each of us must exercise judgment about which lies we will tell, which weaknesses we will exploit, or what sort of compensation—cash, cocktails, a fistful of flash drives—we feel we are entitled to (in a culture that values success over ethics, the virtuous worker has become an anomaly).

Judgment is our moral compass confronting our desires and revealing which pull within us is stronger. No one navigates a day without saying—whether in word or deed—that this is better than that, or that more right than this. Fluffing our views with phrases like "not that I'm judging or anything" does not change the truth any more than saying, "with all due respect" before showing none.

Recognizing this reality is one of our great modern predicaments because we've come to cherish the idea that to be judgmental is the only real wickedness. Can this paradox be reconciled? It can. But only if we're willing to acknowledge that we are all in denial about how judgmental we really are.

Who me?? Yes, you.

At the root of our new **judgment** paradox is the fact that we've adopted a gold standard for thinking that says let's leave God out of it, but fail to see we've created a far more imperious god: Me & Mine. We who wanted to make our own rules, our own standards for right and wrong, have created a culture that is infinitely more judgmental than the law of the Lord (which fully recognizes our very human tendency to want things our own way, and endeavors to help us—the great big world of us—navigate these challenges together).

This is the essential difference between judgment with or without God in the picture. **The law of the Lord** (aka the law of us) is holistic in nature. Under this law you are asked to consider a point of view other than the one that most appeals to you. The law of Me & Mine makes no such demands, a condition that suits us just fine. Until it doesn't. Until we find ourselves longing for a kind of happiness we can't seem to get to on your own.

Remember, happiness is built primarily on purpose and meaning, and purpose and meaning are a match of our heart's desire and the world's deep need. Needs don't exist in the abstract—they represent the poverty of people's lives: material, spiritual, relational. There are many kinds of needs but no significant happiness that doesn't involve being interwoven in the mess and joy of others, and no significant meaning without our gifts going to serve some purpose bigger than ourselves.

We use that expression a lot—*some bigger purpose*—without really talking about the larger implications. Like, where did it come from—this purpose—this reason for being or doing that is somehow bigger than each one of us, and yet includes us all? Whose vision was it? And how does it get disseminated from age to age? Our very happiness depends on this purpose—this meaning—but we can't seem to connect the dots back to the source. If we could, we'd likely find that the happiness we seek is just on the other side of this nod: there is a God, and Me & Mine are not it.

But when the psalmist says **the** judgment, isn't he talking about fire and brimstone and all that stuff? This judgment day idea has been poorly served throughout history by the human desire to gain power through fear mongering, and lately, through the perfect storm of fear mongering and big screen entertainment. At first glance, **will not stand** conjures up popular images of a rendered verdict, i.e., *will not be able to stand up to scrutiny*.

In truth, it's not scrutiny that determines our fate but rather our own willfulness. Every year of our brief lives, God is calling to us with his very flesh. Those who've made a habit of rejecting his overtures may find their proud resistance so deeply embedded they can't—won't—reverse themselves. Their final wishes—to have no part of God—will, therefore, be honored for eternity.

But, but, what about heaven? This question rises up like a child's plea, asking for something there is no logical reason to expect or demand. The psalmist, whose role is to teach the way the world works, would find the argument curious—like asking for the final scene of a play to be resolved in a way that is completely inconsistent with the words and deeds and expressed beliefs of the characters throughout.

If we spend any time with this psalm we will likely see that **will not stand** carries another meaning: *choose not to stand.* This is a common posture in the 21st century: I reject the whole premise of God's judgment and therefore none of this applies to me. I choose not to participate. I choose not to play your game. Like a child covering his eyes and declaring someone else invisible.

The trouble is, without God in the picture we become our own judges. We alone carry the burden of worrying about the toll of our secret pleasures, and their ripple effect of pain. Of knowing our words—or lack of them—have crushed people's spirits, and will live on in them after we're gone. Of bargaining with the failing air in our lungs over whatever good we did in the world, and whether or not it counted.

Perhaps because we judge ourselves so harshly it's easy to believe that God does, too, but the psalmist says nothing about "being good enough for heaven." This wisdom prayer simply teaches that if we long for the sort of happiness that endures we need only to meditate on his law. To listen, yield, follow, love. This is the language of grace inviting us to discover **the way** where the burden of worthiness and climbing are lifted like a bright soap bubble, and all that is left to do is look skyward in **delight**.

But what if there is no God, no heaven? What would be the point to any of this? This is an area of great confusion and needs to be set right if we're going to apply this ancient wisdom to modern life. An endgame called Heaven is not the point of God. You are. You and me and who we were created to be, love, and serve, and all the providential moments that await us along **the way** where pride dies to love and sets us free—now and straight through to forever.

If there is no God then this is an abiding poem of lies. If there is no God then there is no path to happiness because modern social science has proven that happiness comes primarily from meaning and purpose and we have no way of understanding these values without an overarching lens of beneficence and interdependence. If there is no God, then the whole idea of gifts and passions and *being born to do just this* is just something we made up. If there is no God, then all we have is the advice of the wicked and we might as well take it because—why not? What else is there, right? Might as well enjoy it.

Except, somehow, we don't. As the levels of anxiety, depression, addiction, anger, loneliness, and fear metastasize in the 21st century far beyond anything that human history has ever imagined, we look to everything but the Living God for answers.

"We would rather be ruined than changed," says the poet W.H. Auden. This is the heart of the human dilemma, and it is both modern and eternal.

###

Therefore the wicked
will not stand in the judgment

nor sinners
in the congregation
of the righteous

Misery loves company. When we've fallen into the trap of perpetual self-gratification, we look for others who are in it, too. This reassures us that we're not so bad, that our struggles are normal, that maybe it's really those other people over there pretending to be happy who've got it all wrong. In the throes of urges and actions that might prompt someone to say to us stop!, we tend to steer clear of the sorts of people we imagine might say it.

We tell ourselves that **the righteous** don't understand the sorts of driving urges that we—the ones with the true appetite for living or the loftier sense of duty—have. We throw up our best defense: that we feel judged. We comfort ourselves with the delusion that those with happy little lives must come by it naturally, and keep our distance in case the truth is otherwise.

But put us all in a room with no place to hide and get ready for what the culture calls a real "come to Jesus" moment. The sudden realization by all of us who stand divided by social or political or spiritual matters that our struggle with *wanting what the heart wants* is universal, that we all fall short, and that our feelings of being on the outside—unworthy, unlovable—are less about other people's judgment and more about our not being quite ready to give up whatever it is at the root of our misery.

Let's face it: we simply don't like to spend much time with people who value different things, or hold different values than our own. It's too uncomfortable, too threatening. As certain as we are that we are right, we can never be certain enough.

New parents experience this profoundly as their lives widen and the choices they make for their own families begin to impact their circle of relationships. Friends who decide to quit smoking weed after the baby comes will likely stop hanging out as much with friends who continue. A mom who believes that "boys will be boys" will stop setting play dates with mothers who find rough housing to be a character issue. The husband who still enjoys a bachelor lifestyle when he travels on business will soon find his friend who's gone freelance to be home with the kids dull, and a bit prudish. And the method of feeding these 21st-century infants? Well, this stirs a level of righteous indignation unheard of in human history.

Our modern interpretation of the word **righteous** has only added to the rift. For the past thousand-plus years, to be righteous was a compliment of the highest order. It meant to be good. Good, as in *just*; good, as in a person you could count on to be fair in all things. A righteous man was one who resisted the natural tendency to favor the rich and the powerful, who did not let those who were swift of tongue bully those who could not express themselves as clearly, who considered the poor and the vulnerable to be human beings deserving of equal consideration.

A righteous man knows how to yield not because it's always easy or natural, but because the **law of the Lord** teaches him that his happiness is inversely affected by the amount of unhappiness he causes others. Feelings of guilt, shame, and remorse are not, as it turns out, a hot house for happiness. Those who believe they have somehow transcended those burdensome feelings are, if Bronnie Ware is to be believed, in for a rude awakening.

Our sense of the word **congregation** has narrowed considerably, too. In the realm of the psalmist, it would have meant an assembly of God's people coming together, but there were no walls, no fixed location; just people with a common heart drawing nearer to the voice that said, "let's gather round."

Today, **congregation** is used almost exclusively to mean *church*, and righteous to mean **self**-righteous. The pairing of these two word pictures has had sweeping effects in the modern world, sequestering those who like it that way, and depriving the rest of us of the life-giving marrow of **righteousness**. In its stead, we have lifted up tolerance as the highest form of love.

Now tolerance is better than intolerance, to be sure, but when the marginalized or the demonized or the innocent cry out, tolerance doesn't have what it takes to save them. Why not? Because tolerance is passive. Love is active.

Righteous love demands sacrifices no one would ever make without believing they are a part of something greater than themselves. That this interconnection is somehow bigger than our own likes and dislikes. That what looks like renouncing our own privilege might actually be the very door to our heart's desire. Wherever the righteous congregate, they, like trees planted, are invited to learn the quiet joy of being someone else's shade.

This is an invitation that the sinner wants no part of.

###

For the LORD watches over the way of the righteous

Well, that doesn't seem fair. If God is supposedly good then he should watch over all of us, shouldn't he? Just because we don't want him to tell us what to do or not to do—or even believe in him at all—doesn't mean he shouldn't still have our backs. Believing this with all our hearts, we shun the well-lit path, opt for a dead-end alley, and dare God to protect us anyway.

Sure, it sounds like we're trying to have it both ways, and yes, we know that this defies all logic and reason, and yet—somehow—we proceed as if nothing is impossible with God. We can't help ourselves. Having someone to watch over us is a primal desire for the telling moments of our lives to be credited or forgiven. Our very natures seem to require some sort of just oversight, if not from God, then from the people we believe can guide, protect, promote, reward, or sympathize with us in his stead. Time and again we are disappointed to find that no human being can live up to our expectations. Still the longing never leaves us.

How did it get there, this longing? And why would we have a universal template for it in our psyches if this idea were not writ large somehow in the universe?

If pondering the word **delight** revealed to us that it is the flashpoint of our desire for meaning being drawn to the source of meaning itself, then might it be that our desire for someone to watch over our lives and deem us worthy is a response to the source of the one who gives us value?

We're getting warmer. Let's return to the verse for a second:

The Lord watches over
the righteous

That's what is says, right? No, but that's how our competitive ears tend to hear it because, well, if God plays favorites then who needs him, right? But God doesn't play favorites. We are the ones who tend to skim over the key phrase: **the way**.

The Lord watches over
the way of the righteous

The way is what we begin to follow when we stop heeding the advice of the wicked, rise up out of the scoffer's seat, and begin leaning into a new voice. **The way** is what teaches us who we are, what we're really like, and who we were meant to be. **The way** is not new or even ancient, but rather, eternal, running straight through from one side of life to the other.

Called by some the highway of God, it invites us to follow a dome of light that reveals little more than our next steps—*just trust me*—as we're called into the One who dwells like a circumference around all time and space and us.

The Way

Centuries before the psalmist wrote of the two ways, an ancient prophet named Isaiah cried out in the wilderness, "prepare **the way** of the Lord." Centuries after the psalmist wrote these words, Jesus revealed that he was "**the way**, the truth, and the life." That he'd come to heal, teach, suffer, die, and rise because the thing *he was born to do* was to become the mysterious and living way for all people to be reconciled to God for the remainder of time.

Can you even imagine such a thing? Not really, right?

Yet the history of the world continues to record what has been true for the past eighty generations; that people who never thought they'd believe in a way of life named Jesus, somehow, changed their minds. And their hearts were made new, and their faith as strong as if they'd been there from the very first, gathered with those who'd sat at His feet, and were called, aptly, people of **The Way**.

In the end, the first psalm is an echo of the grand narrative of Life being told by God in flesh and blood. Through Jesus, and through us. Which is why this wisdom verse ends with the sure assertion that:

the way of the wicked
will perish.

We already know this, don't we? Our minds and our loins may not want anything to do with religion, but our heart knows how the story ends: good triumphs over evil. We may have forgotten why this is or how it came to be, but the truth abides in us nonetheless.

We know it when we see it. Why else would we flock to the big screen to watch epic battles played out to their glorious conclusions? We are ravenous for stories of heroes and villains and unlikely saints who save the world in the nick of time because no matter the era or armor or plight, we know that they are we, and we are insatiable for that single ending that will satisfy the human heart.

The difference between fiction and reality is that on the screen the good guys and the bad guys are more clearly defined. Real life is more complicated, the advice of the wicked often harder to recognize—or resist.

If only there were evil people somewhere insidiously committing evil deeds, and it were necessary only to separate them from the rest of us and destroy them. But the line dividing good and evil cuts through the heart of every human being. And who is willing to destroy a piece of his own heart?"

—Aleksandr Solzhenistyn

This Nobel Prize-winning novelist dares to say what the modern world will not: that we are all sinners, and there's no real hope for happiness until we can own that. That's it. That's all. Grace can take it from there. Grace, that is love incarnate, says you don't need to keep trying to prove yourself—not to Me or to anyone else. You can't rewrite the ending because it's already been written. Whatever needs fixing, we can do it together. Here, let me show you what I mean.

> You show me the path of life,
> in your presence there
> is fullness of joy.
> (Psalm 16:11)

In the mid 1900s, an English professor named C. S. Lewis wrote the classic tale of good and evil called *The Chronicles of Narnia.* He also meditated a great deal on this matter of happiness, just as you are doing now. In considering the two paths, he came up with this advice for the forward thinking among us: "We all want progress, but if you're on the wrong road, progress means doing an about-turn and walking back to the right road; in that case, the man who turns back soonest is the most progressive."

Today, we imagine that progress means leaving behind the baggage of old teaching. Happiness is freedom we shout, but find that we are neither happy nor free. For all the freedom our modern life provides, the burden to prove ourselves in it has proved soul crushing.

We may be confused by this paradox but Jesus is not. His words like an outstretched hand transcend time and circumstance to speak to the troubled heart of man:

> "Come to me all who are weary and burdened and I will give you rest."
>
> (Matthew 11:28)

Take the verse in. Meditate on it. Consider how intimate the phrase "come to me" is. And the word *all*? How does it align with whatever you know or think about Jesus?

Take some time with *weary* and *burdened*. Is this how you feel—some days, most days? How did you come to be this way? What were the forces or faces or beliefs that led to this heaviness—this deep need for rest in your soul? How might this idea of rest relate to freedom? And how might this kind of freedom differ from what we experience in our modern lives of individualism and infinite choice?

You might ponder this for a day or a week or a lifetime. There's no rush. You have arrived at a place of rest. Of the peace that passes all human understanding. Of Jesus.

And happy are those who accept His invitation.

###

About the author

Heather Choate Davis began her writing career as an advertising copywriter. Over the past 30 years, she's written screenplays, teleplays, one-acts, liturgies, and books. She's taught creative writing, created an arts-based vespers called The Renaissance Service TM, and led retreats at a high desert monastery. Davis has her MA in Theology from Concordia University, Irvine, and is the co-founder of a company called icktank. You can find out more about her writing, work, and passion projects at heatherchoatedavis.com. Davis lives with her husband, Lon, in Mar Vista, CA. The psalms and the ancient prayer practice of *lectio divina* are dear to her heart. She leaves you with this promise: "For freedom Christ has set us free." (Galatians 5:1)

Wisdom is meant to be shared.
When you're done with this book,
please pass it along.

64364596R00080

Made in the USA
Lexington, KY
06 June 2017